WHY NUCLEAR DISARMAMENT MATTERS

WHY
NUCLEAR
DISARMAMENT
MATTERS

Hans Blix

A Boston Review Book

THE MIT PRESS Cambridge, Mass. London, England

MIT Press books may be purchased at special quantity
discounts for business or sales promotional use. For
information, please e-mail special_sales@mitpress.mit.edu or
write to Special Sales Department, The MIT Press,
55 Hayward Street, Cambridge, MA 02142.

This book was set in Adobe Garamond by *Boston Review*
and was printed and bound in the United States of America.

This book was made possible in part by a grant from Carnegie
Corporation of New York. The statements made and views
expressed are solely the responsibility of the author.

Library of Congress Cataloging-in-Publication Data
Blix, Hans.
    Why Nuclear Disarmament Matters / Hans Blix.
    p.   cm. — (Boston Review books)
    ISBN: 978-0-262-02644-4 (alk. paper)
    1. Nuclear disarmament. 2. Nuclear nonproliferation.
    3. Arms control. I. Title
JZ5665.B55 2008
327.1'747—dc22   2007050399

10   9   8   7   6   5   4   3   2   1

*This book is dedicated to the young
generations, who must make their world
more livable by tackling the issues
of disarmament and security.*

CONTENTS

WHY
NUCLEAR
DISARMAMENT
MATTERS

1

SIXTY YEARS AGO I WAS A STUDENT at the University of Uppsala in Sweden. World War II had just ended, the United Nations had been established, and we had great hopes of creating a better and more peaceful world. Our optimism was soon dashed. The Iron Curtain descended and the Cold War began, lasting nearly 45 years. It would be wrong to say that no progress was made during this period: trade and communications skyrocketed; science and technology leapt forward; human rights became a universal global concern; scores of countries won their independence; the gap between rich and poor countries was recognized as unacceptable; U.N. organizations developed as instruments for global cooperation between states; environmental hazards were recognized; and a fair amount of arms control was achieved in spite of everything. However, the threat of more than 50,000 nuclear warheads capable of destroying human civilization hung over the world.

The end of the Cold War, and of the ideological division of the world, raised hopes again for a new era of global cooperation. It was expected that arms control and disarmament would become easier after the end of the Cold War, but after some initial successes we have been disappointed. During the Cold War the American and Soviet nuclear arsenals would have sufficed to destroy human civilization several times over. Public opinion mobilized against the madness of the arms race, and despite the intense political and ideological competition, each superpower accepted some limitations on itself in order to achieve limitations on the other and on other states generally. But in recent years, with no serious territorial or ideological conflicts between the major military powers, and as states of the world have come together to face environmental and health threats, the climate for arms control and disarmament has, amazingly, deteriorated.

There are warnings that the 1968 Nuclear Non-Proliferation Treaty—the global instrument through which states declared themselves against the acquisition of nuclear weapons and for nuclear disarmament—is now in danger. The good news is that the world is not replete with would-be violators. The overwhelming commitment to the treaty remains tremendously valuable: Libya and Iraq were both found to be in violation and brought back into observance. In two other cases—North Korea and Iran—the world is actively seeking solutions. For now, at least, there appear to be no other problematic cases.

Still, the dangers are real and the treaty is under strain. The global process of arms control and disarmament has stagnated in the last decade; it needs to be revived and pursued in tandem with efforts to prevent the spread of weapons of mass destruction to more states and to terrorist movements.

Although reductions are taking place in overstocked nuclear arsenals, these are still estimated to number some 27,000 weapons; the reduction is in redundancy only. What is even worse, the commitments to further disarmament made by the nuclear-weapon states in 1995, when the non-nuclear-weapon states agreed to extend the Non-Proliferation Treaty and their pledges indefinitely, are being ignored. Meanwhile, efforts to consolidate global treaties have stalled. Not surprisingly, the 2005 review conference of the Non-Proliferation Treaty ended in bitterness with many non-nuclear-weapon states feeling cheated. Negotiations have not even opened on the much-needed treaty to stop the production of fissile material for weapons.

In the last few years we have even been moving backwards. Several nuclear states no longer give pledges against first use of nuclear weapons. North Korea has tested a nuclear weapon and many governments suspect Iran of developing the capacity to enrich uranium in pursuit of nuclear weapons. The United Kingdom announced that it will take steps allowing a new nuclear weapons program, and the Bush administration has declared its wish to prepare for the production of a new kind of nuclear weapon—the Bombplex—reportedly to the tune of $150 billion and probably more. Meanwhile, the U.S. administration has plans for installations in Poland and the Czech Republic as part of a missile shield. These plans worry the Russian government, which finds it hard to believe—or to persuade the Russian population—that these installations on Russia's doorstep are meant only to guard against possible future Iranian (and North Korean) missiles.

Moreover, the militarization of space has

long been a fact. There is now the risk that weapons could be stationed in space, hanging over us like Swords of Damocles. Testing its ballistic missiles, China shot down one of its own satellites, leaving a vast number of hazardous fragments in space, in addition to those created by Soviet and U.S. activities in the 1980s. Yet, until recently, the United States, the United Kingdom, and Israel opposed discussions on arms control in space.

Meanwhile, about $1.3 trillion goes into the world's military expenses annually; about half of this is from the United States.

In spite of all this, governments and the public are paying less attention to the global regimes for arms control and disarmament. One reason is the intense and justified focus on measures against terrorism and the handling of specific cases of actual or potential nuclear proliferation. Another reason may be that global treaties did not help to prevent the 9/11 terrorist attacks on the United States. The treaties also constituted insufficient barriers against the efforts of Iraq, North Korea, and Libya to acquire nuclear weapons, and against Iran's efforts to conceal a program for the enrichment of uranium.

While the reaction of most states to the treaty violations was to seek to strengthen and develop existing treaties and institutions, the United States, the sole superpower, has looked more to its own military might for remedies. The U.S. National Security Strategy of 2002 made it clear that the United States would feel free to use armed force, without the authorization of the U.N. Security Council, to counter not only an actual or imminent attack involving weapons of mass destruction, but also a threat that might be uncertain as to time and place. The aim of the strategy, reaffirmed in 2006, is said to be "to help make the world not just safer but better," indicating that the United States believes that this new policy has benefits for all.

No one underestimates the difficulties on the road to disarmament and to outlawing nuclear weapons in the same manner that other weapons of terror—biological and chemical weapons—have been outlawed. Some of the current stagnation in global arms control and disarmament forums results from a paralyzing requirement of consensus combined with an outdated system of bloc politics. A more important impediment, however, is that the nuclear-weapon states no longer seem to take their commitment to nuclear disarmament seriously—even though this was an essential part of the Non-Proliferation Treaty bargain, both at the treaty's birth in 1968 and when it was extended indefinitely in 1995.

Despite these discouraging signs, it is possible to glimpse light at the end of the tunnel. True, the devaluation of international commitments inherent in these positions risks undermining the credibility and effectiveness of multilateral treaty commitments. But against a generally gloomy short-term outlook for arms control and disarmament, some positive developments can be discerned in the broader field of security. The number of armed conflicts between states has been declining. Peacekeeping operations have prevented and continue to prevent conventional wars in many places. Efforts to reform the U.N. have borne some fruit and more may be hoped for. The new U.N. Peace Building Commission will assist states emerging from conflicts, thereby reducing the risk of their relapse into violence.

The Security Council recently passed an important resolution obligating member states to adopt domestic legislation designed to prevent the proliferation of weapons of mass destruction. The precedent is constructive. But if the Council were to further use and develop its quasi-legislative potential, it would need to ensure that it acts with the broad support of U.N. members. In the long run, this would entail making the Council more representative of the U.N. membership.

In today's rapidly integrating world community, global treaties and global institutions, like the U.N., the International Atomic Energy Agency (IAEA), and the Organization for the Prohibition of Chemical Weapons, remain indispensable. Even with their shortcomings they can do some important things that states acting alone cannot achieve. They are, therefore, essential instruments in the hands of the international community to enhance security, jointly operate inspection systems, and reduce the threat of weapons of mass destruction. Governments that have shown disenchantment with global treaties and institutions will, I believe, inevitably return and renew their engagement.

The call to action, in fact, has already been sounded. During the first months of 2003, the late Swedish Foreign Minister, Anna Lindh, phoned me from time to time seeking information about the U.N. inspection work in Iraq, for which I was responsible. She and many of her colleagues were very unhappy about the drift towards military action against Iraq and felt that the inspectors should be given more time for their search for weapons of mass destruction. She also felt, however, that opposition to armed counter-proliferation action had to be matched by other active policies on the issue of non-proliferation. I fully agreed with her and was pleased to see that in June 2003 she and her colleagues in the European Union declared new joint policies.

These policies, in my view, started from sensible premises: that the best solution to the problem of the proliferation of weapons of mass destruction is that countries should no longer feel that they need them and that violators should be encouraged to walk back and rejoin the international community. These policies stressed the need for a cooperative approach to collective security and a rule-based international order. They highlighted the role of international verification and effective multilateralism. They also supported, as a last resort, however, the position that coercive measures under Chapter VII of the U.N. Charter could be taken, with the Security Council as the final arbiter.

By the end of June 2003, when the occupation of Iraq was a fact and I was leaving the U.N., Anna Lindh contacted me again. She thought that the time was right not only for the new European policies but also for an idea first advanced by Jayantha Dhanapala, then U.N. Under-Secretary-General for Disarmament: the creation of an independent international commission to examine how the world could tackle the problem of weapons of mass destruction. She asked if I would chair such a commission. I said I would. After Anna Lindh's death, the Swedish Prime Minister, Göran Persson, and Anna's successor as Foreign Minister, Laila Freivalds, gave me a free hand to establish the Weapons of Mass Destruction Commission.

In the spring of 2006, the commission presented its unanimous report, "Weapons of Terror," to U.N. Secretary-General Kofi Annan. The report urged governments to wake up from what Annan has called their "sleepwalking" and revive arms control and disarmament. When there is a greater general readiness to return to a cooperative multilateral system in the sphere of arms control and disarmament, the commission's report, excerpted at the end of this book (available in full at http//www.wmdcommission.org), will, I hope, contribute to the practical agenda. Some ideas and recommendations are new, but the commission also argues in favor of some well-known existing proposals.

Indeed, at the present time it seems to me that not only successes in the vital work to prevent proliferation and terrorism but also progress in other areas could transform the current gloom into hope. Bringing the Comprehensive Nuclear-Test-Ban Treaty into force would significantly impede the development of new nuclear weapons. The weapons that exist today are bad enough. Negotiating a global treaty to stop the production of fissile material for weapons would dry up the source for new such material and help hinder possible arms races, notably in Asia. In both of these areas the United States has decisive leverage. If it takes the lead, the world is likely to follow. If it does not take the lead, there could be more nuclear tests and new nuclear arms races.

2

THE YEARS 2006 AND 2007 WILL NOT GO down in history as the years of disarmament, but perhaps as the years when it was realized that achieving disarmament by war and democracy by occupation is difficult, and that we must resume our efforts to revive disarmament through cooperative actions and negotiations.

When considering how to reduce the current threat of nuclear weapons, it is necessary to look back at the two basic approaches the world has taken: international norms stipulating a general prohibition on the use of force; and norms outlawing specific weapons or their use. Let's take one at a time, starting with international law concerning the use of force.

Since World War II there has been a tremendous consolidation and expansion of international law in general. Customary law has been codified. Trade, finance, and communications have prompted thousands of treaties. Space, nuclear energy, and human rights are new spheres subject to international law. The fabric of law of the international community is getting wider and stronger and helps us to avoid conflicts. However, rules restricting the use of armed force have been less reliable.

Some would say that it is as naïve today as ever to think that the use of armed force between states could be subject to meaning-ful legal restrictions. Is it really? The world is changing and restrictions that once appeared naïve are perhaps no longer absurd as rules guiding the conduct of states. The use of armed force between states of the European Union is today considered unthinkable. However, before I discuss the present, allow me a quick flashback.

Writing about five hundred years ago, Machiavelli (1492–1550), as one might expect, did not call for any restrictions. He wrote, "That war is just which is necessary and every sovereign entity may decide on the occasion for war." In the nineteenth century, the right to go to war was still not challenged. However, views were beginning to change. It was commonly stressed that war should be a means of last resort, and prohibitions on the use of particularly cruel weapons, like the dum-dum bullet, started to come into force.

The twentieth century saw two world wars but also efforts to build collective security and global institutions. The states party to the Kellogg-Briand Pact of 1928 formally renounced war as a means of national policy, and the Covenant of the League of Nations affirmed the duty to try to settle disputes by peaceful means. The notion was developing that war was not permitted except in self-defense. These efforts failed. World War II broke out, only twenty years after the end of the first.

The Charter of the U.N., drafted at San Francisco in 1945 in the wake of the devastation of World War II and the U.S. nuclear attacks on Nagasaki and Hiroshima, marked a leap forward in the world's thinking about the use of armed force. The authors agreed on a general prohibition of the threat or use of force between members. Article 2:4 of the Charter stipulated that members must refrain from the threat or use of force against the territorial integrity and political independence of any state. The rule was not just an exhortation: under Chapter VII the Security Council was authorized to take measures, including military action, when it determined that there was a threat to the peace, a breach of the peace, or an act of aggression. In Article 25, member states agreed to accept and carry out such decisions of the Council.

In practical terms, upholding the ban on the use of armed force was made dependent on the five victors in World War II (the United States, the United Kingdom, France, China, and the Soviet Union), who were permanent members of the Council and whose consent was needed for all decisions of substance. As we know, the collective security system of the U.N. was mostly paralyzed because of the veto power used by the United States and the Soviet Union. States could not expect to be protected by the Council, but had, as before, to protect themselves through individual or collective self-defense, a right that was explicitly preserved in Article 51. I quote: "Nothing in the present Charter shall impair the inherent right of individual or collective self-defense if an armed attack occurs against a Member of the United Nations, until the Security Council has taken measures necessary to maintain international peace and security." On paper the reliance on the "inherent" right of individual or collective self-defense looked like an exception. The sad reality was that during the Cold War the collective security system of the U.N. Charter was mostly inoperative.

After the end of the Cold War and the collapse of Communism, the security situation changed drastically. In the Security Council, consensus between the five permanent members became possible. The most important U.N. action taken in the new political climate was, of course, the authorization by the Security Council for the broad alliance created by President George H. W. Bush to intervene in 1991 to stop Iraq's naked aggression against and occupation of Kuwait. For some time this successful action gave hope to the world that the five great powers at long last had the will to make the Charter work as originally envisaged. President Bush spoke of "a new world order."

In 2003, however, a number of states launched the war in Iraq without the authorization of the Security Council. Indeed, they were aware that their action would not obtain the Council's authorization. The political justification given for the Iraq war was above all the contention that Iraq retained or was developing weapons of mass destruction in direct violation of Security Council resolutions. It was the first time a full-scale armed intervention was taken in the name of enforcing the non-proliferation of nuclear weapons. It is unlikely that any other argument would have persuaded the U.S. Congress or the U.K. Parliament to authorize armed action. As we know, the evidence was faulty, but the states launching the war ignored the reports of the U.N. Monitoring, Verification and Inspection Commission, which I led, and the International Atomic Energy Agency.

The armed action in Iraq in 2003 has generally been considered a violation of the U.N. Charter rules on the use of force. However, it was in line with the U.S. National Security Strategy published in September 2002. This paper states flatly that, in the era of missiles and terrorists, a limitation on the right to use armed force in self-defense in cases where "armed attacks" are occurring or are "imminent" is unacceptable. As I see it, the 2002 strategy report and the 2003 war show that the U.S. administration said goodbye to the restrictions that the United States had helped to formulate in San Francisco on the use of force, at least as regards actions to stop the development of weapons of mass destruction.

The U.S. administration may have thought of itself as a global sheriff, able, unlike the U.N., to act responsibly and forcefully to avert threats. I quote the U.S. National Defense Strategy of 2005: "The end of the Cold War and our capacity to influence global events open the prospects for a new and peaceful system in the world." Another quote from the same document shows that the administration views "international fora"—including, one would assume, the U.N.—mainly as obstacles on the road to this peaceful system. I quote again: "Our strength as a nation will continue to be challenged by those who employ a strategy of the weak using international fora, judicial processes, and terrorism." The U.S. administration has not explained whether it feels bound by any international limitation on the use of armed force. The former U.S. ambassador to the U.N., John Bolton, clearly did not think so. In 2003 he wrote: "Our actions, taken consistently with Constitutional principles, require no separate, external validation to make them legitimate."

Before the war on Iraq in 2003, Dr. Condoleezza Rice said that you don't have to wait for a "mushroom cloud" before taking military—preemptive or preventive—action, and she has also been reported to have argued that the United States would be justified in taking action in "self-defense" against Iran. One is driven to the conclusion that the right to take unilateral preemptive or preventive action is deemed to arise long before an armed attack occurs and a mushroom cloud appears. Indeed, it would seem to arise even when the first milligrams of low-enriched uranium come out of a cascade of centrifuges. Is the administration giving itself a completely free license to take police action against "rogue states" with nuclear programs, or any other kind of armed action? If so, does it accord the same right to other states?

It remains to be seen whether in practice the United States and its future administrations will again be ready to use armed force that is neither in response to an armed attack nor authorized by the Security Council. In any case, one must conclude that at present a question mark hangs over the effectiveness of the San Francisco rule—at least as far as the United States is concerned.

How worrisome is it when Article 51 of the U.N. Charter is seen as irrelevant by the strongest military power in the world? The restrictions on the use of force in the Charter are only some sixty years old, and for most of their existence the rules were inoperative and frequently ignored. They were in deep freeze during the Cold War, but they thawed in 1991. Moreover, Article 51 of the U.N. Charter does not require a country to delay self-defense until the arms have struck. It is generally agreed that if bombers or missiles are approaching and an attack is imminent, the state under attack may take armed action, without asking the Security Council for permission. A problem inherent in all self-defense taken before an attack is even imminent (and visible) is that it is based on intelligence. Since 2003, we know that this can be a very shaky ground on which to start a war. Iraq in 2003 was not about to attack the United States, nor any other country. Unsurprisingly, the majority of the world's governments have not endorsed the wide, unilateral license to invoke the kind of "self-defense" used to justify the armed action in Iraq.

The question nevertheless remains of at which point unilateral action becomes justified. Is the generally accepted "imminence" of an armed attack today too restrictive a criterion? There is no serious discussion of this question at the governmental level today. The argument can reasonably be made that if an armed attack is not imminent, there would be time to go to the Security Council, which would have the authority, under existing Charter rules, to decide on action if it determined that there was a "threat to international peace and security."

It is important to note that, unlike a state, the Security Council can take or authorize enforcement measures not only when attacks are imminent but as soon as it determines that there is a "threat to international peace and security." The spectrum of measures includes economic and military sanctions and, under Article 25 of the U.N. Charter, member states agree "to accept and carry out" such Chapter VII decisions. Thus, whenever the Council, including the permanent members, is able to agree that there is a threat to the peace, it has enormous power to decide on measures that are binding to all members.

But what is a "threat to the peace"? In 1991, when the Council met at the summit level, a presidential statement made on behalf of the full Council declared that "the proliferation of all weapons of mass destruction constitutes a threat to international peace and security." The statement should be interpreted, I think, as a signal that the Council was ready in the future, "in cases of proliferation," to decide on measures that could be binding. In 2004 the Council made interesting use of this authority. In resolution 1540 it affirmed that "proliferation of nuclear, chemical and biological weapons, as well as their means of delivery, constitutes a threat to international peace and security." On the strength of this determination the Council decided, with binding effect for all members, that all states shall *inter alia* adopt laws prohibiting non-state actors from engaging in the production and acquisition of weapons of mass destruction.

By this resolution the Security Council clearly moved from concrete threats raised by specific cases of proliferation to potential threats arising from a large number of possible unidentified actions. Member states were ordered to enact legislation to reduce the risk of proliferation flowing from such actions.

Resolution 1540 raises hopes for an invigorated Security Council. At the same time, some caution is needed. The Council, already both judge and executive authority, makes itself legislator with this resolution.

The presidential statement in 1991 and Resolution 1540 did not point to any specific situation as constituting a "threat to the peace." However, in neither case did the Security Council require member states to take any measures of enforcement. The case of Iran, now before the Security Council, may be different. It may involve economic and other enforcement measures. While some Council members remain convinced that Iran's ambition to enrich uranium is part of an effort to develop a nuclear weapon option, to "proliferate," in a number of years time, it would be hard to claim that such ambition, if it is there, constitutes a threat to international peace and security today.

The U.N. Charter authors who emerged from World War II were not pacifists. They were also not trigger-happy. We should learn from them. It was truly worrisome that in the case of Iraq, the United States claimed the right of self-defense to justify armed action to eliminate weapons of mass destruction that did not exist. It would be a further great setback for the world if the United States were to dump the U.N. Charter restrictions on the unilateral use of armed force and recognize a right of self-defense against the threat of some milligrams of low-enriched uranium and possible intentions to proliferate in a number of years time. Fortunately, at the time of this writing, the risk of a resort to armed action against Iran seems to have receded.

What can we do? We might welcome a Security Council that is made more representative of today's world, acts in tune with it, and requests that all U.N. members take some action to reduce potential future threats to the peace. Council decisions on concrete enforcement actions, however, should be limited to situations that really are urgent: where there is an acute, not just a potential, threat to the peace. For all other situations, the authors of the U.N. Charter wisely wrote Chapter VI, calling for the peaceful settlement of disputes, "the continuation of which is likely to endanger the maintenance of international peace and security."

3

Before the establishment of the U.N. Charter prohibiting the threat or use of force generally, the international community's early approach to weapons of mass destruction was simply to ban their specific use—as, for example, in the 1925 Geneva Protocol against bacteriological and chemical weapons.

A later approach embraced the idea that the best way to guarantee against a weapon's use is to ensure that it is not produced, or if it is produced that it is not acquired, or if it is produced and acquired that it is not stockpiled. Thus, in 1946 the General Assembly declared its determination to eliminate the production of "atomic weapons" and other weapons of mass destruction. But this approach—arms control treaties—faced problems of monitoring and enforcement: while violations of a ban on use would, in all likelihood, be visible, a violation of a ban on production and stockpiling could be hidden. To be reliable the new approach required inspection.

The authors of the Biological Weapons Convention of 1972, an initiative of President Nixon, took an important step beyond the 1925 Geneva Protocol by prohibiting the production and stockpiling of biological weapons, but during the Cold War they were unable to agree on mechanisms for verification and inspection. At the time, the Soviet Union would not accept any on-site inspection. We now know that this weakness enabled the Soviet Union to develop a large biological weapons program in violation of the convention, and that Iraq under Saddam Hussein did the same in the 1980s. This weakness remains. In 2001 the United States rejected a verification regime, which included on-site inspection. A review conference in late 2006 raised some hope that a new multifaceted approach may be worked out to strengthen the convention.

Steps were also taken to address chemical weapons. The Chemical Weapons Convention was concluded in 1993 after decades of negotiations. Chemical weapons had been used on many occasions, including Saddam Hussein's use of them on a large scale in the war with Iran and, indeed, against Iraq's own Kurdish citizens. The convention comprises an inspectorate, both to supervise the destruction of stocks of chemical weapons and to monitor chemical industries. Large-scale destruction of stocks has taken place in the United States, Russia, and other countries. Stocks remaining in Iraq after the Gulf War were destroyed under the supervision of U.N. inspectors.

But we have not been able to achieve rules specifically banning the production, stockpiling, and use of nuclear weapons. No comprehensive treaty ban like the Biological Weapons Convention and the Chemical Weapons Convention has been accepted. Nor did the advisory opinion of the International Court of Justice in 1996 outlaw their use in all circumstances: it recognized a limited scope for a legal use of nuclear weapons.

Nonetheless, pressures since the 1960s have pushed in that direction. During the Cold War people marched in the streets out of the fear that a U.S.-Soviet nuclear exchange would lead to global catastrophe. There was anguish, and although the approach of governments was fragmentary, a good deal of action was taken to reduce the threat. Multilateral agreements prohibited placing nuclear weapons in the Antarctic, on the seabed, or in outer space. A partial test-ban treaty, concluded in 1963, stopped the testing of nuclear weapons in the atmosphere and thereby prevented further radioactive fallout. Important bilateral agreements were reached between the two military superpowers to reduce the risks: the "hot lines" between Moscow and Washington established in the wake of Cuban Missile Crisis, when the world realized just how close it had come to nuclear war; and in 1969, and later in the 1970s, the Strategic Arms Limitation Treaty, which first froze the number of missile launchers and then set goals for reducing the number of nuclear missiles.

The key agreement, however, is the Non-Proliferation Treaty of 1968. It aimed to achieve a nuclear-weapon-free world through a double bargain: all non-nuclear-weapon states were invited to renounce nuclear weapons and accept international inspection. The five nuclear-weapon states at the time (the United States, the United Kingdom, France, the Soviet Union, and China) were invited to commit themselves to negotiations toward nuclear disarmament and to facilitate the transfer of nuclear technology to non-nuclear-weapon states. In many respects it has been a very successful treaty. All states in the world have adhered to it, with the exception of India, Pakistan, and Israel, which have all developed nuclear weapons. North Korea withdrew from the treaty in 2002. On the other hand, Byelorussia, Kazakhstan, and the Ukraine transferred the nuclear weapons they had to Russia, and South Africa dismantled its nuclear weapons.

The Non-Proliferation Treaty is under strain today because non-nuclear-weapon states have over the years become increasingly dissatisfied that the nuclear-weapon state parties are not moving seriously toward disarmament. Moreover, the ambition to induce India, Pakistan, and Israel to adhere has been abandoned. Nuclear-weapon states claim to have lived up to their treaty obligations by reducing their stockpiles, and point to Iraq and Libya, which violated the treaty with programs to develop nuclear weapons. (These violators were brought back into compliance.)

Some in the United States argued that arms control treaties and international verification were of little value as they were respected by the "good guys" and ignored by the "bad guys." Nevertheless, in 1995 the Non-Proliferation Treaty was prolonged indefinitely and the nuclear-weapon states reaffirmed the obligations they had undertaken to negotiate toward disarmament. Without that commitment, the prolongation would not have been approved.

With that agreement came great hopes that the world would, indeed, move toward disarmament and more effective international cooperation. But that hope has been dashed again and again: the projected treaty prohibiting production of more highly enriched uranium and plutonium for weapons has stalled, and no progress has been made to eliminate nuclear weapons in the Middle East. A treaty comprehensively banning nuclear weapons tests was adopted in 1996, but it was rejected by the U.S. Senate, and so long as the United States refrains from binding itself, several other states (China, for example) will do the same and there will be only an uncertain moratorium.

In 2005, the review conference of the Non-Proliferation Treaty could not even agree on a final declaration. Nuclear-weapon states brushed aside the commitments they had made in 1995 and 2000. Non-nuclear-weapon states felt cheated and blocked agreement on other matters. It ended with stalemate. The U.N. General Assembly Summit later in 2005 could not agree to put a single line about disarmament or non-proliferation in its declaration, and the Conference on Disarmament in Geneva has not been able even to agree on a work program for some ten years.

Is there any hope for new or strengthened arms control treaties in this climate? Do "rogue states" and terrorists render any kind of international agreement about disarmament useless? In the view of the WMD Commission, arms control and disarmament treaties are essential, but we must understand what makes them work.

Most importantly, states must be ensured security without nuclear weapons. In most cases of non-adherence to and non-compliance with the Non-Proliferation Treaty, the report of the WMD Commission observes, "perceived threats to security have been the incentive for the acquisition of nuclear weapons and security guarantees of various kinds have offered disincentives." I would add that convincing states that they do not need weapons of mass destruction would be significantly easier if all U.N. members practiced genuine respect for the existing restraints on the threat and use of force.

In all cases of noncompliance, the commission stressed the need to understand why states seek to acquire weapons of mass destruction, and the need to work to remove the incentives. In addition to perceived security needs, demands for recognition seem to be an important motive. Recognition and status may be important to governments that, for various reasons, have been isolated: for example, Libya, North Korea, and Iran. Libya divested itself of its nuclear program following negotiations that led to enhanced official recognition and the lifting of U.N.

sanctions. In the case of North Korea, former President Jimmy Carter's visit to President Kim Il Sung in 1994 opened the door to an agreement. A current offer of non-attack and a normalization of relations with the United States and Japan may help to finalize it. In the case of Iran, diplomatic relations exist with all the negotiating parties except the United States. Although an American offer of security guarantees and a normalization of relations could carry great weight, no such offers have been extended.

What will convince a state that its security will be served by a credible renunciation of nuclear weapons? One approach taken by the Bush administration (especially with Iran) has been to convey the message that moving toward nuclear weapons will actually jeopardize security—that it will result in increased isolation and vulnerability and may trigger Security Council intervention or armed preventive counter-proliferation action by the United States.

One difficulty with this approach is that "rogue states" may seek to move faster toward nuclear weapons in the belief that this will help to deter counter-proliferation. Another problem concerns legality and legitimacy: a state's technological progress toward nuclear-weapon capability, while worrisome, does not constitute an "armed attack" that justifies the use of armed force under the U.N. Charter. The Security Council, although entitled to authorize military action against a "threat to the peace," seems unlikely to go that far to eliminate alleged or apparent WMD programs that are not actively used as threats.

Hence, especially in the wake of the horrendous consequences of military action in Iraq, both the Council and member states are likely to avoid military action in favor of political, diplomatic, and economic measures.

If military action is ruled out, can the opposite—positive guarantees of security—be persuasive as an incentive to stop or forgo nuclear programs? In the case of North Korea, the Bush administration seems to think so. As part of a deal, and perhaps to meet North Korea's stated concern about the "hostile attitude" of the United States, guarantees against attack from the outside appear to be offered. For Iran, however, security guarantees have not been on the table, although it is hard to believe that such guarantees would have no useful effect, given U.S. military presence in the region and the Bush administration's policies of regime change.

Security is of central importance to all Middle Eastern states. Attempts to verify the claim that Iran's enrichment program aims only to produce fuel will not reduce concerns. Aims can change over time, and the cold fact is that the very existence of an industrial-scale enrichment plant in Iran with the potential to produce weapons-grade uranium would likely increase tension in the region. Practically all parties would want to see a negotiated agreement under which Iran suspended the enrichment program and was rewarded for this. Rewards could consist of security guarantees, a normalization of relations, and support for its program to use nuclear power.

I have suggested that offering North Korea and Iran assurances in the security field could be one important element to induce them to accept deals in the nuclear field. Among the U.N. member states, would general measures of arms control and disarmament in the nuclear field facilitate the talks with North Korea and Iran? Negotiations with Iran, especially, will not be easy under any circumstances, but I suspect that they might be somewhat less difficult if the nuclear-weapon states could show that their requests are part of a broader effort to lead the world, including themselves, toward nuclear disarmament. Preventing further proliferation is essential, but it is not a recipe for success to preach to the rest of the world to stay away from the very weapons that nuclear states claim are indispensable to their own security.

Moreover, the Security Council's current demand that Iran suspend its enrichment program as a precondition for talks is humiliating, and it is no surprise that Iran has rejected it. Failure in the case of Iran could create serious risks of escalation and long-term domino effects. Will the nuclear powers, and especially the United States, take new approaches?

This brings me to my main message, which is that fulfillment by all parties of the bargain underlying the Non-Proliferation Treaty is required if the treaty is to remain viable. It is not a treaty that appoints the nuclear-weapon states individually or jointly to police non-nuclear-weapon states and to threaten them with punishment. It is a contract in which all parties commit themselves to the goal of a nuclear-weapon-free world. If police action is to take place, it must be authorized by the Security Council in conformity with the U.N. Charter. The nuclear-weapon states party to the Non-Proliferation Treaty have a strong voice in the Council, but they are not alone.

Practically all the non-nuclear-weapon states have fulfilled and are fulfilling their part of the Non-Proliferation Treaty contract with great positive effects on security and stability in the world. The nuclear-weapon states should help move the world to a further globalization not only of economy and development, but also of security.

4

It is said that before the United States took action to secure the secession of Panama from Colombia about a hundred years ago, President Theodore Roosevelt asked his Attorney General whether a legal argument should be made to justify the action. The high legal official replied: "Mr. President, why let such a beautiful operation be marred by any petty legal considerations?"

In recent years some have told us again that you can in effect ignore international humanitarian law or restrictions in the

U.N. Charter at will. You can, but the cost of doing it is higher today than a hundred years ago.

A crucial mark of a civilized society is that the citizens have given up the personal possession of arms and conferred upon public authorities a monopoly on the right to possess and use arms in accordance with law. Societies must travel a long road to reach this stage, and the road remains bumpy in many places. In the international community, states continue to possess their own arms and the possibility of using them. We need to identify and promote changes that will transform this community of individually armed states into a society in which the states have disarmed drastically, and common institutions control the use of force in accordance with agreed rules.

We undoubtedly have a long way to go,

but there are some hopeful signs.

After Iraq there is a growing understanding that military power and pressures may not be the best way to enforce non-proliferation. The Bush administration is showing greater interest in diplomacy, for instance in the case of North Korea, and greater interest in using the Security Council.

Another encouraging sign: in January 2007 a group of U.S. elder statesmen—former Secretaries of State George Shultz and Henry Kissinger, former Secretary of Defense William Perry, and former Senator Sam Nunn—published an editorial in *The Wall Street Journal* titled "A World Free of Nuclear Weapons." These seasoned Cold War statesmen urged the United States to launch a "major effort," first and foremost in "intensive work with the leaders of the countries in possession of nuclear weapons," to "turn the goal of a world without nuclear weapons into a joint enterprise." What, more specifically, should the nuclear-weapon states be asked to do? Dr. Kissinger and his co-authors point to fulfillment of the Non-Proliferation Treaty bargain. During the Cold War, they say, nuclear weapons were necessary for deterrence. Today they are not needed between the big powers and the enduring arsenals may be an incentive for others, including terrorists, to acquire such weapons.

A similar message emerged from the United Kingdom. In a letter that accompanied the white paper of December 4, 2006 on the United Kingdom's nuclear weapons program, the Foreign Secretary, Margaret Beckett, wrote: "We stand by our unequivocal undertaking to accomplish the total elimination of nuclear weapons and we will continue to press for multilateral negotiations toward mutual, balanced and verifiable reductions in nuclear weapons."

I note as a further hopeful sign that the talks with North Korea have come to be pursued with more inducements and fewer threats, an approach that is more likely to get results. Regrettably, we do not yet see any similar posture vis-à-vis Iran, where the threats have been loud.

The commission that I headed stressed that when we want to convince states to stay away from or do away with nuclear weapons, the best approach is that which makes the states feel they do not need nuclear weapons for their security. Hearing big powers talk about the development of new nuclear weapons, or insist that all options are on the table, does not create such feelings.

With accelerating interdependence,

there is an increasing necessity to cooperate in order to protect the global environment, to manage the global economy, and to stop the spread of contagious diseases. Why not also cooperate to stop killing each other?

Gorbachev wrote recently—rightly—about "a failure of political leadership, which proved incapable of seizing the opportunities opened by the end of the Cold War." So it will be the task of this generation to help move the world to real peace—to revive disarmament and to replace armed force with dialogue and diplomacy.

What would a broad program of global disarmament look like? While the WMD Commission pleaded for a convention outlawing nuclear weapons similar to the conventions outlawing biological and chemical weapons, there are many more modest steps that could and should be taken without much delay.

Let me sketch some of the recommendations of the WMD Commission, starting with three system-level measures.

The Conference on Disarmament in Geneva, the principal international forum for negotiation on issues related to weapons of mass destruction, has been unable to adopt an agenda for almost a decade. As a result, during this time no substantive issues have been discussed or negotiated in the conference. This stalemate is the unsatisfactory result of a consensus requirement that has its roots in Cold War practices. The conference should be able to make administrative and procedural decisions, including the adoption of a program of work, by a qualified majority of two thirds of the membership present and voting. This would not guarantee results but it would at least guarantee that the important issues be discussed between governments.

Given the setbacks in arms control and disarmament at the Non-Proliferation Treaty review conference and the U.N. summit in 2005, we need to reset the stage for a credible multilateral disarmament and non-proliferation process. The General Assembly should convene a new World Summit on disarmament, non-proliferation, and the use of weapons of mass destruction by terrorists. Since thorough preparations would be necessary, planning should start as soon as possible.

Alongside these system-level measures, the commission proposes many substantive measures to reduce the risk of proliferation of nuclear weapons and the dangers of existing arsenals.

No measure could be more urgent—important in substance and as a signal that arms control and disarmament are again on the world agenda—than the signing and ratification of the Comprehensive Nuclear-Test-Ban Treaty by states that have not yet done so. If the treaty were seen to lapse, there would be an increased risk that some state might restart weapons tests. Demanding that North Korea ratify the treaty—which is necessary for the treaty to enter into force—would be easier if all the states participating in the six-power talks had themselves ratified the treaty. Ten years have been lost. There is no time to continue keeping the treaty in limbo.

The next most urgent task is to negotiate without further delay a treaty prohibiting the production of fissile material for weapons. A continued reduction in the number of existing nuclear weapons and a verified closing of the tap for more enriched uranium and plutonium for weapons would gradually reduce the world inventory of bombs. A draft of a cutoff treaty has been presented in Geneva. It has crucial weaknesses—notably, the absence of a provision for international verification—but it should be welcomed as a draft and discussed.

Such a treaty, to be meaningful, must provide for effective international verification. We know that verification is possible. Independent international verification of enrichment and reprocessing plants is already carried out by the European Atomic Energy Community (EURATOM) in two nuclear-weapon states, France and the United Kingdom. Enrichment plants in Brazil and Japan are subject to International Atomic Energy Agency safeguards verification. If there is no effective international verification, any controversy about respect for the treaty would have to be discussed on the basis of evidence that came only from national means of verification. We know from the case of Iraq that this would not be satisfactory. Without independent verification, suspicions of violations might arise and lead to a race between some countries in the production of fissile material.

In addition, steps taken by all nuclear-weapon states to reduce strategic nuclear arsenals would be significant as confidence-building measures. The United States and Russia, which have the most weapons, should take the lead. Russia, in a climate of increasing cooperation with the European Union, should withdraw nuclear weapons from forward deployment to central storage, and the United States should withdraw nuclear weapons from Europe to American territory.

All states that have nuclear weapons should commit themselves categorically to a policy of no first use, and the United States and Russia should reciprocally take their nuclear weapons off hair-trigger alert.

If reliance on nuclear power increases, as is expected, the need for greater production of low-enriched uranium fuel and for the disposal of larger quantities of spent fuel can be anticipated. This must occur in a manner that does not increase the risk of proliferation, or of diversion of material to "rogue states" or terrorists. Various proposals are on the table, and international arrangements that ensure the availability of nuclear fuel for civilian reactors while minimizing the risk of weapons proliferation should be explored. The International Atomic Energy Agency is the most suitable forum for such exploration. The production of highly enriched uranium should be phased out. It has very limited use.

Regional approaches will also be needed, especially in sensitive areas. A zone free of weapons of mass destruction in the Middle East, first proposed by Egypt and Iran in 1974, has universal support in the region. However, while such a zone may well be an indispensable part of a broader peace settlement, it is not realistic in the present political and security climate.

Arrangements to limit the number of enrichment and reprocessing plants in particularly sensitive areas might be an alternative option. In the De-nuclearization Declaration of 1992, the two Korean states agreed between themselves that neither would have enrichment or reprocessing plants on its territory. Any new nuclear arrangement for the peninsula is expected to include this feature.

Could the Korean model be followed by the states of the Middle East? In the past year several have voiced interest in developing nuclear power, and some observers fear that sensitive nuclear-fuel-cycle facilities could also be contemplated. Such facilities would surely increase tension. Security Council Resolution 687 (1991) characterized the elimination of Iraq's capability to enrich uranium as a step toward a nuclear-weapon-free zone in the Middle East. Perhaps commitments could be made by all states in the region to forgo the enrichment of uranium and reprocessing of plutonium for a prolonged period of time in exchange for guarantees of fuel-cycle services from elsewhere. Such an agreement would not touch existing quantities of enriched uranium or plutonium, whether in laboratories, stores, or Israeli weapons. But if such an agreement were subject to effective international inspection, it might constitute a practical and confidence-building first step on the long and difficult road to a nuclear-free zone in the Middle East.

Meanwhile, controls on radioactive and fissionable material should be strengthened everywhere to impede trafficking and make it harder for terrorists to acquire such material.

Lastly, international professional inspection, as practiced under the U.N., the International Atomic Energy Agency, and the Chemical Weapons Convention, is an important and effective tool for verification. Such inspection does not conflict at all with national means of verification.

Rather, these two fact-finding methods supplement each other. International verification systems have legal access to installations, records, and people. International intelligence employs a host of surveillance techniques. Many states, though, have no national means at their disposal and should not have to be dependent upon the intelligence of other states. States that do operate such intelligence may, in one-way arrangements, provide information to the international verification systems. The reports of the international systems offer governments a chance for a quality check on their national systems and corroboration of their conclusions.

The international community must revive disarmament and take advantage of the resources the U.N. offers. For some twenty years the window that opened at the end of the Cold War has been allowed to hang flapping in the wind. It is high time that the five nuclear-weapon states take seriously their commitment to negotiate toward nuclear disarmament. It would have a dramatic impact on the world political climate and reduce incentives to nuclear proliferation. And it could lead to a cooperative security order. The U.N. must play a central role in this order. It remains a vital instrument, while not the only one, and the Charter provides the fundamental guidelines, which should be respected. As Dag Hammarskjöld said, the U.N. will not take us to heaven but it might help us to avoid hell.

APPENDIX

RECOMMENDATIONS OF THE WEAPONS OF
MASS DESTRUCTION COMMISSION

*Preventing the proliferation of nuclear
weapons*

1. All parties to the Non-Proliferation
Treaty need to revert to the fundamental
and balanced non-proliferation and
disarmament commitments that were made
under the treaty and confirmed in 1995
when the treaty was extended indefinitely.

2. All parties to the Non-Proliferation Treaty should implement the decision on principles and objectives for non-proliferation and disarmament, the decision on strengthening the Non-Proliferation Treaty review process and the resolution on the Middle East as a zone free of nuclear and all other weapons of mass destruction, all adopted in 1995. They should also promote the implementation of the "thirteen practical steps" for nuclear disarmament that were adopted in 2000.

3. To enhance the effectiveness of the nuclear non-proliferation regime, all Non-Proliferation Treaty non-nuclear-weapon state parties should accept comprehensive safeguards as strengthened by the International Atomic Energy Agency Additional Protocol.

4. The states party to the Non-Proliferation Treaty should establish a standing secretariat to handle administrative matters for the parties to the treaty. This secretariat should organize the treaty's review conferences and their preparatory committee sessions. It should also organize other treaty-related meetings upon the request of a majority of the state parties.

5. Negotiations with North Korea should aim at achieving a verifiable agreement including, as a principal element, North Korea's manifesting its adherence to the Non-Proliferation Treaty and accepting the 1997 Additional Protocol, as well as revival and legal confirmation of the commitments made in the 1992 Joint Declaration on the De-nuclearization of the Korean Peninsula: notably, that neither North nor

South Korea shall have nuclear weapons or nuclear-reprocessing and uranium-enrichment facilities. Fuel-cycle services should be assured through international arrangements. The agreement should also cover biological and chemical weapons, as well as the Comprehensive Nuclear-Test-Ban Treaty, thus making the Korean peninsula a zone free of weapons of mass destruction.

6. Negotiations must be continued to induce Iran to suspend any sensitive fuel-cycle-related activities and ratify the 1997 Additional Protocol and resume full cooperation with the International Atomic Energy Agency in order to avoid an increase in tensions and improve the outlook for the common aim of establishing a Middle East zone free

of weapons of mass destruction. The international community and Iran should build mutual confidence through measures that should include: reliable assurances regarding the supply of fuel-cycle services; suspending or renouncing sensitive fuel-cycle activities for a prolonged period of time by all states in the Middle East; assurances against attacks and subversion aiming at regime change; and facilitation of international trade and investment.

7. The nuclear-weapon states party to the Non-Proliferation Treaty should provide legally binding negative security assurances to non-nuclear-weapon state parties. The states not party to the Non-Proliferation Treaty that possess nuclear weapons should separately provide such assurances.

8. States should make active use of the IAEA as a forum for exploring various ways to reduce proliferation risks connected with the nuclear fuel-cycle, such as proposals for an international fuel bank; internationally safeguarded regional centers offering fuel-cycle services, including spent-fuel repositories; and the creation of a fuel-cycle system built on the concept that a few "fuel-cycle states" will lease nuclear fuel to states that forgo enrichment and reprocessing activities.

9. States should develop means of using low-enriched uranium in ships and research reactors that now require highly enriched uranium. The production of highly enriched uranium should be phased out. States that separate plutonium by reprocessing spent nuclear fuel should explore possibilities for reducing that activity.

10. All states should support the international initiatives taken to advance the global clean-out of fissile material. Such support should encompass the conversion of research reactors from highly enriched to low-enriched uranium fuel, storing fissile material at centralized and secure locations and returning exported nuclear materials to suppliers for secure disposal or elimination.

11. All Non-Proliferation Treaty nuclear-weapon states that have not yet done so should ratify the protocols of the treaties creating regional nuclear-weapon-free zones. All states in such zones should conclude their Comprehensive Safeguards Agreements with the IAEA and agree to ratify and implement the Additional Protocol.

12. All states should support continued efforts to establish a zone free of weapons of mass destruction in the Middle East as a part of the overall peace process. Steps can be taken even now. As a confidence-building measure, all states in the region, including Iran and Israel, should commit themselves for a prolonged period of time to a verified arrangement not to have any enrichment, reprocessing or other sensitive fuel-cycle activities on their territories. Such a commitment should be coupled with reliable assurances about fuel-cycle services required for peaceful nuclear activities. Egypt, Iran, and Israel should join the other states in the Middle East in ratifying the Comprehensive Nuclear-Test-Ban Treaty.

13. India and Pakistan should both ratify the Comprehensive Nuclear-Test-Ban Treaty and join those other states with nuclear weapons that have declared a moratorium on the production of fissile material for weapons, pending the conclusion of a treaty. They should continue to seek bilateral détente and build confidence through political, economic, and military measures, reducing the risk of armed conflict, and increasing transparency in the nuclear and missile activities of both countries. Eventually, both states should become members of the Nuclear Suppliers Group and the Missile Technology Control Regime, as well as parties to IAEA safeguards agreements under the terms of the 1997 Additional Protocol.

Preventing nuclear terrorism

14. States must prevent terrorists from gaining access to nuclear weapons or fissile material. To achieve this, they must maintain fully effective accounting and control of all stocks of fissile and radioactive material and other radiological sources on their territories. They should ensure that there is personal legal responsibility for any acts of nuclear terrorism or activities in support of such terrorism. They must expand their cooperation through *inter alia* the sharing of information, including intelligence on illicit nuclear commerce. They should also promote universal adherence to the International Convention for the Suppression of Acts of Nuclear Terrorism and to the Convention on the Physical Protection of Nuclear Material and implementation of U.N. Security Council resolution 1540.

Reducing the threat and the numbers of existing nuclear weapons

15. All states possessing nuclear weapons should declare a categorical policy of no first use of such weapons. They should specify that this covers both preemptive and preventive action, as well as retaliation for attacks involving chemical, biological, or conventional weapons.

16. All states possessing nuclear weapons should review their military plans and define what is needed to maintain credible non-nuclear security policies. States deploying their nuclear forces in triads, consisting of submarine-launched missiles, ground-based intercontinental ballistic missiles and long-range bombers, should abandon this practice in order to reduce nuclear-weapon redundancy and avoid fuelling nuclear arms races.

17. Russia and the United States should agree on reciprocal steps to take their nuclear weapons off hair-trigger alert and should create a joint commission to facilitate this goal. They should undertake to eliminate the launch-on-warning option from their nuclear war plans, while implementing a controlled parallel decrease in operational readiness of a large part of their strategic forces, by:

• reducing the number of strategic submarines at sea and lowering their technical readiness to launch while in port;

• storing nuclear bombs and air-launched cruise missiles separately from relevant air fields;

• storing separately nose cones and/or warheads of most inter-continental ballistic missiles or taking other technical measures to reduce their readiness.

18. Russia and the United States should commence negotiations on a new strategic arms reduction treaty aimed at reducing their deployments of strategic forces allowed under the Moscow Treaty on Strategic Offensive Reductions by at least half. It should include a legally binding commitment to irreversibly dismantle the weapons withdrawn under the Moscow Treaty. The new treaty should also include transparent counting rules, schedules and procedures for dismantling the weapons, and reciprocal measures for verification.

19. Russia and the United States, followed by other states possessing nuclear weapons, should publish their aggregate holdings of nuclear weapons on active and reserve status as a baseline for future disarmament efforts. They should also agree to include specific

provisions in future disarmament agreements relating to transparency, irreversibility, verification, and the physical destruction of nuclear warheads.

20. All states possessing nuclear weapons must address the issue of their continued possession of such weapons. All nuclear-weapon states party to the Non-Proliferation Treaty must take steps toward nuclear disarmament, as required by the treaty and the commitments made in connection with the treaty's indefinite extension. Russia and the United States should take the lead. Other states possessing nuclear weapons should join the process, individually or in coordinated action. While Israel, India, and Pakistan are not parties to the Non-Proliferation Treaty, they, too, have a duty to contribute to the nuclear disarmament process.

21. Russia and the United States should proceed to implement the commitments they made in 1991 to eliminate specific types of non-strategic nuclear weapons, such as demolition munitions, artillery shells, and warheads for short-range ballistic missiles. They should agree to withdraw all non-strategic nuclear weapons to central storage on national territory, pending their eventual elimination. The two countries should reinforce their 1991 unilateral reduction commitments by developing arrangements to ensure verification, transparency, and irreversibility.

22. Every state that possesses nuclear weapons should make a commitment not to deploy any nuclear weapon, of any type, on foreign soil.

23. Any state contemplating replacement or modernization of its nuclear-weapon systems must consider such action in the light of all relevant treaty obligations and its duty to contribute to the nuclear disarmament process. As a minimum, it must refrain from developing nuclear weapons with new military capabilities or for new missions. It must not adopt systems or doctrines that blur the distinction between nuclear and conventional weapons or lower the nuclear threshold.

24. All states possessing nuclear weapons, notably Russia and the United States, should place their excess fissile material from military programs under IAEA safeguards. To facilitate the reduction of stocks of highly enriched uranium, states possessing such stocks should sell urani-

um blended to enrichment levels suitable for reactor fuel to other Non-Proliferation Treaty states or use it for their own peaceful nuclear energy needs.

25. All states possessing nuclear weapons should adopt strict standards for the handling of weapons-usable fissile material deemed to be in excess of military requirements or recovered from disarmament activities, as exemplified in the U.S. stored-weapon and spent-fuel standards.

26. The Conference on Disarmament should immediately open the delayed negotiations for a treaty on the cutoff of production of fissile material for weapons without preconditions. Before, or at least during, those negotiations, the

Conference on Disarmament should establish a group of scientific experts to examine technical aspects of the treaty.

27. To facilitate fissile material cut-off negotiations in the Conference on Disarmament, the five Non-Proliferation Treaty nuclear-weapon states, joined by the other states possessing nuclear weapons, should agree among themselves to cease production of fissile material for weapon purposes. They should open up their facilities for such production to IAEA safeguards inspections, building on the practice of EURATOM inspections in France and the United Kingdom. These eight states should also address the issue of verifiable limitations of existing stocks of weapons-usable nuclear materials.

28. All states that have not already done so should sign and ratify the Comprehensive Nuclear-Test-Ban Treaty unconditionally and without delay. The United States, which has not ratified the treaty, should reconsider its position and proceed to ratify the treaty, recognizing that its ratification would trigger other required ratifications and be a step towards the treaty's entry into force. Pending entry into force, all states with nuclear weapons should continue to refrain from nuclear testing. Also, the 2007 conference of Comprehensive Nuclear-Test-Ban Treaty signatories should address the possibility of a provisional entry into force of the treaty.

29. All signatories should provide financial, political, and technical support for the continued development and operation

of the verification regime, including the International Monitoring System and the International Data Center and its secretariat, so that the Comprehensive Nuclear-Test-Ban Treaty Organization is ready to monitor and verify compliance with the treaty when it enters into force. They should pledge to maintain their respective stations and continue to transmit data on a national basis under all circumstances.

From regulating nuclear weapons
to outlawing them

30. All states possessing nuclear weapons should begin planning for security without nuclear weapons. They should start preparing for the outlawing of nuclear weapons through joint practical and incremental measures that include definitions, benchmarks, and transparency requirements for nuclear disarmament.

BOSTON REVIEW BOOKS

Boston Review Books are accessible, short books that take ideas seriously. They are animated by hope, committed to equality, and convinced that the imagination eludes political categories. The editors aim to establish a public space in which people can loosen the hold of conventional preconceptions and start to reason together across the lines others are so busily drawing.

Indianapolis
Marion County
Public Library

Renew by Phone
269-5222

Renew on the Web
www.imcpl.org

For General Library Information
please call 269-1700